POETRY FROM CRESCENT MOON

Selections from the *Vita Nuova*

Selections From the *Vita Nuova*

Dante Alighieri

Translated by Thomas Okey
Edited by Joanna Finn-Kelcey

CRESCENT MOON

First published 2000. Second edition 2008. Revised edition 2016.
Translation © Thomas Okey and J.M. Dent 1906.
Introduction, Notes and Bibliography © Joanna Finn-Kelcey
2000, 2008, 2016.

Printed and bound in the U.S.A..
Set in Garamond Book 10 on 14pt.
Designed by Radiance Graphics.

British Library Cataloguing in Publication data

Dante Alighieri, 1265-1321
Selections from the Vita Nuova – (European Writers Series)
1. Dante Alighieri, 1265-1321 – Translations into English
I. Title II. Finn-Kelcey, Joanna

851.1

ISBN-13 9781861711526
ISBN-13 9781861715401

Crescent Moon Publishing
P.O. Box 1312
Maidstone, Kent
ME14 5XU, U.K.
www.crmoon.com

CONTENTS

ACKNOWLEDGEMENTS

To J.M. Dent (London) for *The Vita Nuova and Canzoniere of Dante Alighieri*, translated by Thomas Okey (J.M. Dent, 1906).

Selections from the *Vita Nuova*

Henry Holiday, Dante and Beatrice

Gustave Doré, Dante and Beatrice, from The Divine Comedy

II

Nove fiate già, appresso al mio nascimento, era tornato lo cielo della luce quasi ad un medesimo punto, quanto alla sua propria girazione, quando alli miei occhi apparve prima la gloriosa donna della mia mente, la quale fu chiamata da molti Beatrice, i quali non sapeano che si chiamare.

Ella era già in questa vita stata tanto, che nel suo tempo lo cielo stellato era mosso verso la parte d'oriente delle dodici parti l'una d'un grado: si che quasi dal principio del suo anno nono apparve a me, ed io la vidi quasi alla fine del mio nono. Ella apparvemi vestita d'un nobilissimo colore umile ed onesto, sanguigno, cinta ed ornata alla guisa che alla sua giovanissimia etade si convenia. In quel punto dico veracemente che lo spirito della vita, lo quale dimora nella segretissima camera del cuore, cominciò a tremare sì fortemente, che aparia ne' menomi polsi orribilmente; e tremando disse queste parole: *Ecce Deus fortior me, qui veniens dominabitur mihi.*

In quel punto lo spitiro animale, il quale dimora nell' alta camera, nella quale tutti li spiriti sensitivi portano le loro percezioni, si cominciò a maravigliare molto, e parlando spezialmente allo spirito del viso, disse queste parole: *Apparuit jam beatitudo vestra.* (II)

III

...che questa mirabile donna aparve a me vestita di colore bianchissimo, in mezzo di due gentili donne, le quali erano di più lunga etade; e passando per una via, volse gli occhi verso quella parte ov'io era molto pauroso; e per la sua ineffabile cortesia, la quale è oggi meritata nel grande secolo, mi salutò molto virtuosamente tanto, che mi parve allora vedere tutti i termini della beautitudine.

L'ora, che lo suo dolcissimo salutare mi giunse, era fermamente nona di quel giorno: e perocchè quella fu la prima volta che le sue parole si mossero per venire a' miei orecchi, presi tanta dolcezza, che come inebbriato mi partii dalle genti, e ricorso al solingo luogo d'una mia camera, e puosimi a pensare di questa cortesissima.

E pensando di lei, mi sopraggiunse un soave sonno, nel quale m'apparve una maravigliosa visione: che mi parea vedere nella mia camera una nebula do colore di fuoco, dentro alla quale io discernea una figura d'uno Signore, di pauroso aspetto a chi lo guardasse. E pareami con tanta letizia, quanto a sè, che mirabil cosa era: e nelle sue parole dicea molte cose, le quali io non intendea se non poche, tra le quali io intendea queste: *Ego dominus tuus*. Nelle sue braccia mi parea vedere una persona dormire nuda, salvo che involta mi parea in un drappo sanguigno leggiermente; la quale io riguardando molto intentivamente, conobbi ch'era la donna della salute, la quale m'avea lo giorno dinanzi degnato di salutare. E nell'una delle mani mi parea che questi tenesse una cosa, la quale ardesse tutta; e pareami che mi dicese queste parole: *Vide cor tuum*. E quandoegli era stato alquanto, pareami che disvegliasse questa che dormia; e tanto se sforzava per suo ingegno, che le facea mangiare quella cose che in mano gli ardeva, la quale elle mangiava dubitosamente. Appresso ciò, poco dimorava che la sua letizia si convertia in amarissimo pianto: e così piangendo si ricogliea questa donna nelle sue braccia, e con essa mi parea che se ne gisse verso il cielo: ond' io sostenea si grande angoscia, che le mio deboletto sonno non potè sostenere, anzi si ruppe, e fui disvegliato. Ed immantinente cominciai a pensare; e trovai che l'ora, nella quale m'era questa visione apparita, era stata la quarta della notte: sì che appare manifestamente, ch'ella fu la prima ora delle nove ultime ore della notte.

[...]

A ciascun' alma presa, e gentil core,
Nel cui cospetto viene il dir presente,
A ciò che mi riscrivan suo parvente,
Salute in lor signor, cioè Amor.

Già eran quasi ch' atterzate l'ore
Del tempo che ogni stella n'è lucente,
Quando m'apparve Amor subitamente,
Cui essenza membrar mi dà orrore.

Allegro mi sembrava Amor, tenendo
Mio core in mano, e nelle braccia avea
Madonna, involta in un drappo dormendo.

Poi la svegliava, e d'esto core ardendo
Lei paventosa umilmente pascea:
Appresso gir ne lo vedea piangendo.

XIII

Tutti li miei pensier parlan d'amore,
Ed hanno in lor sì gran varietate,
Ch'altro mi fa voler sua potestate,
Altro folle ragiona il suo valore:

Altro sperando m'apporta dolzore:
Altro pianger mi fa spesse fïate;
E sol s'accordano in chieder pietate,
Tremando di paura ch'è nel core.

Ond'io non so da qual materia prenda;
E vorrei dire, e non so ch'io mi dica:
Così mi trovo in amorosa erranza.

E se con tutti vo' fare accordanza,
Convenemi chiamar la mia nemica,
Madonna la pietà, che mi difenda.

XV

Se io non perdessi le mie virtudi, e fossi libero tanto ch'io potessi rispondere, io le direi, che sì tosto com' io immagino la sua mirabil bellezza, sì toto mi giugne un desderio di vederla, il quale è di tante virtude, che uccide e distrugge nella mia memoria ciò che contra lui si potesse levare; e però non mi ritraggono le passate passioni da cercare la veduta di costei. Ond' io, mosso da cotali pensamenti proposi di dire certe parole, nelle quali, scusandomi a lei di cotal riprensione, ponessi anche quello che mi addiviene presso di lei; e dissi questo sonetto:

Ciò, che m'incontra nella mente more
Quando vegno a veder voi, bella gioia,
E quand'io vi son presso, sento Amore,
Che dice: 'Fuggi, se 'l perir t'è noia,

Lo viso mostra lo color del core,
Che, tramortendo, ovunque può s'appoi;
E per l'ebrietà del gran tremore
Le pietre par che gridin: 'Moia, moia.'

Peccato face chi allor mi vide,
Se l'alma sbigottita non conforta,
Sol dimostrando che de me gli doglia,

Per la pietà, che 'l vostro gabbo uccide,
La qual si cria nella vista smorta,
Degli occhi, c' hanno di lor morte voglia.

XVI

Spese fiate venemi alla mente
L'oscura qualità ch'Amor mi dona;
E vienmente pietà si, che sovente
Io dico: 'ahi lasso! avvien egli a persona?'

Ch' Amor m'assale subitanamente
Sì, che la vita quasi m'abbandona:
Campami un spirito vivo solamente,
E quei riman, perchè di voi ragiona.

Poscia mi sforzo, chè mi voglio aitare;
E così smorto, e d'ogni valor vôto,
Vegno a vedervi, credendo guarire:

E se io levo gli occhi per guardare,
Nel cor mi si comincia uno tremoto,
Che fa da' polsi l'anima partire.

Donna, che' avete intelletto d' amore,
Io vo' con voi della mia donna dire;
Non perch' io creda sue laude finire,
Ma ragionar per isfogar la mente.
Io dico che, pensando il suo valore,
Amor sì dolce mi si fa sentire,
Che, s'io allora non perdessi ardire,
Farei parlando innamorar la gente.
Ed io non vo' parlar s`i altamente,
Che io divenissi per temenza vile;
Ma tratterò del suo stato gentile
A rispetto di lei leggeramente,
Donne e donzelle amorose, con vui,
Chè non è cosa da parlarne altrui.

Angelo chiama in divino intelletto
E dice: 'Sire, nel mondo si vede
Maraviglia nell'atto, che procede
D'un'anima che 'infin qua su risplende.'
Lo cielo, che non have altro difetto
Che d'aver lei, al suo Signor la chiede,
E ciascun santo ne grida mercede.
Sola pietà nostra parte difende,
Chè parla Iddio, che di madonna intende:
'Diletti miei, or soufferite in pace
Che vostra spene sia quanto me piace
Là ov'è alcun che perder lei s'attende,
E che dirà nell' Inferno a' malnati:
'Io vidi la speranza de' beati'.'

Madonna è disiata in altro cielo:
Or vo' di sua virtù farvi savere.
Dico, qual vuol gentil donna parere
Vada con lei, chè quando va per via,
Gitta ne' cor villani Amore un gelo,
Per che ogni lor pensiero agghiaccia e père;
E qual soffrisse di starla a vedere
Diverria nobil cosa, o si morria.
E quando trova alcun che degno sia
Di veder lei, quel prova sua virtute,
Chè gli addivien, ciò che gli da salute.
E si l'umilia, che ogni offesa oblia.
Anor le ha Dio per maggior grazia dato,
Che non può mal finir chi l'ha parlato.

Dice di lei Amor: 'Cosa mortale
Come esser può si adorna e si pura?'
Poi la riguarda, e fra sè stesso giura
Che Dio ne intende di far cosa nova.
Color di perle ha quasi in forma, quale
Conviene a donna aver, non fuor misura:
Ella è quanto di ben può far natura;
Per essempio di lei beltà si prova.
Degli occhi suoi, come ch'ella gli mova,
Escono spiriti d'amore infiammati,
Che fieron gli occhi a qual, che allor gli guati,
E passan si che 'l cor ciascun ritrova:
Voi le vedete Amor pinto nel riso,
Ove non puote alcun mirarla fiso.

Canzone, io so che tu girai parlando
A donne assai, quand t'avrò avanzata.
Or t'ammonisco, perch'io t'ho allevata
Per figliuola d'Amor giovane e piana,
Che dove giugni, tu dichi pregando:

'Insegnatemi gir, ch'io son mandata
A quella, di cui loda io sono ornata.'
E se non vogli andar siccome vana,
Non ristare ove sia gente villana:
Ingégnati, se puoi, d'esser palese
Solo con donna o con uomo cortese,
Che ti merranno per la via tostana.
Tu troverai Amor con esso lei;
Raccomandami a lor come tu déi.

XX

Amore e cor gentil sono una cosa,
Siccom 'il Saggio in suo dittato pone;
E cosi senza l'un l'altro esser osa,
Com' alma razional senza ragione.

Fagli natura, quando è amorosa,
Amor per sire, e 'l cor per sua magione,
Dentro allo qual dormendo si riposa
Talvolta brieve, e tal lunga stagione

Beltate appare in saggia donna pui,
Che piace agli occhi sì, che dentro al core
Nasce un desio della cosa piacente:

E tanto dura talora in costui,
Che fa svegliar lo spirito d'amore:
E simil face in donna uomo valente.

XXIII

Mentre io pensava la mia frale vita,
E vedea 'l suo durar com' è leggiero,
Piansemi Amor nel core, ove dimora;
Per che l'anima mia fu sì smarrita,
Che sospirando dicea nel pensiero:
Ben converrà che la mia donna mora.
Io presi tanto smarrimento allora,
Ch'io chiusi gli occhi vilmente gravati;
Ed eran sì smagati
Gli spiriti miei, che ciascun giva errando.
E poscia immaginando,
Di conoscenza e di verità fuora,
Visi di donne m'apparver crucciati,
Che mi dicen: 'Pur morràti, morràti.'

Poi vidi cose dubitose molte
Nel vano immaginare, ov' io entrai;
Ed esser mi parea non so in qual loco,
E veder donne andar per via disciolte,
Qual lagrimando, e qual traendo guai,
Che di tristizia saettavan foco.
Poi mi parve vedere appoco appoco
Turbar lo Sole ed apparir la stella,
E pianger egli ed ella;
Cader gli augelli volando per l'âre,
E la terra tremare;
Ed uom m'apparve scolorito e fioco,
Dicendomi: 'Che fai? non sai novella?
Morta è la donna tua, ch'era sì bella.'

Levava gli occhi miei bagnati in pianti,
E vedea (che parean pioggia di manna),
Gli angeli che tornavan suso in cielo,
Ed una nuvoletta avean davanti,
Dopo la qual gridavan tutti: 'Osanna';
E s'altro avesser detto, a voi dire' lo.
Allor diceva Amor: Più non ti celo;
Vieni a veder nostra donna che giace.
L'immaginar fallace
Mi condusse a veder mia donna morta;
E quando l'ebbi scorta,
Vedea che donne la covrian d'un velo;
Ed avea seco umiltà sì verace,
Che parea che dicesse: 'Io sono in pace.'

XXVI

Questa gentilissima donna, di cui ragionato è nelle precedenti parole, venne in tanta grazia della genti, che quando passava per via, le persone correano per vederla; onde mirabile letizia me ne giungea. E quando ella fosse presso ad alcuno, tanta onestà venia nel core di quello, ch'egli non ardia di levare gli occhi, nè di rispondere al suo saluto; e di questo molti, siccome esperti, mi potrebbero testimoniare a chi nol credesse. Ella coronata e vestita d'umiltà s'andava, nulla gloria monstrando di ciò ch'ella vedeva ed udiva. Dicevano molti, poi-chè passata era: 'Questa non è femina, anzi è uno de' bellissimi angeli del cielo.' Ed altri dicevano: 'Questa è una meraviglia; che bendetto sia lo Signore che sì mirabilmente sa operare! Io dico ch'ella si mostrava sì gentile e sì piena di tutti i piaceri, che quelli che la miravano comprendevano in loro una dolcezza onesta e soave tanto che ridire nol sapevano; nè alcuno era lo quale potesse mirar lei, che nel principio non gli convenisse sospirare. Queste e più mirabili cose da lei procedeano virtuosamente. Ond'io pensando a ciò, volendo ripigliare lo stile della sua loda, proposi di dire parole, nelle quali dessi ad intendere delle sue mirabili ed eccellenti operazioni; acciocchè non pure coloro che la poteano sensibilmente vedere, ma gli altri sapessono di lei quello che le parole ne possono fare intendere. Allora dissi questo sonetto:

Tanto gentile e tanto onesta pare
La donna mia, quand'ella altrui saluta,
Ch'ogni lingua divien tremando muta,
E gli occhi non ardiscon di guardare.

Ella sen va, sentendosi laudare,
Benignamente d'umilà vestuta;

E par che sia una cosa venuta
Di cielo in terra a miracol mostrare.

Mostrasi si piacente a chi la mira,
Che dà per gli occhi una dolcezza al core,
Che intender non la può chi non la prova.

E par che della sua labbia si muova
Uno spirto soave e pien d'amore,
Che va dicendo all' anima: sospira.

XXXI

Gli occhi dolenti per pietà del core
Hanno di lagrimar sofferta pena,
Sì che per vinti son rimasi omai.
Ora s'io voglio sfogar lo dolore,
Che appoco appoco alla morte mi mena
Convenemi parlar traendo guai.
E perchè mi ricorda ch' io parlai
Della mia donna, mentre che vivia,
Donne gentili, volentier con vui,
Non vo' parlarne altrui,
Se non a cor gentil che 'n donna sia;
E dicerò di lei piangendo, pui
Che se n'è gita in ciel subitamente,
Ed ha lasciato Amor meco dolente.

[...]

Dannomi angoscia li sospiri forte,
Quando il pensiero nella mente grave
Mi reca quella che m' ha il cor diviso:
E spesse fiate pensando la morte,
Me ne viene un desio tanto soave,
Che mi tramuta lo color nel viso.
Quando l'immaginar mi tien ben fiso,
Giugnemi tanta pena d'ogni parte,
Ch'i' mi riscuoto per dolor ch' io sento
E si fatto divento,
Che dalle genti vergogna mi parte.

Poscia piangendo, sol nel mio lamento
Chiamo Beatrice; e dico: 'Or, se' tu morta!
E mentre ch'io la chiamo, mi conforta.

XXXVII

Io venni a tanto per la vista di questa donna, che li miei occhi se cominciaro a dilettare troppo di vederla; onde molte volte me ne crucciava nel mio cuore ed avevamene per vile assai; e più volte bestemmiava la vanità degli occhi miei, e dicea loro nel mio pensiero: Or voi solevate far piangere chi vedea la vostra dolorosa condizione, ed ora, pare che vogliate dimenticarlo per questa donna che vi mira, e che non vi mira se non in quanto le pesa della gloriosa donna di cui pianger solete; ma quanto far potete, fate; chè io la vi rimenbrerò molto spesso, maledetti occhi: chè mai, se non dopo la morte, non dovrebbero le vostre lagrime esser ristate. E quando fra me medesimo così avea detto alli miei occhi, e li sospiri m'assaliano grandissimi ed angosciosi. Ed acciocchè questa battaglia, che io avea meco, non rimanesse saputa pur dal misero che la sentia, proposi di fare un sonetto, e di comprendere in esso questa orrible condizione...

XLI

Oltre la spera, che più larga gira,
Passa il sospiro ch'esce del mio core:
Intelligenza nuova, che l'Amore
Piangendo mette in lui, pur su lo tira.

Quand' egli è giunto là dov' el desira,
Vede una donna, che riceve onore,
E luce si, che per lo suo splendore
Lo peregrino spirito la mira.

Vedela tal, che, quando il mi ridice,
Io non lo intendo, sì parla sottile
Al cor dolente, che lo fa parlare.

So io ch'el parla di quella gentile,
Perocchè spesso ricorda Beatrice,
Sicch' io lo intendo ben, donne mie care.

XLII

Appresso a questo sonetto apparve a me una mirabil visione, nella quale vidi cose, che mi fecero proporre di non dir più di questa benedetta, infino a tanto che io non potessi più degnamente trattare di lei. E di venire a ciò io studio quanto posso, sì com'ella sa veracemente. Sicchè, se piacere sarà di Colui, per cui tutte le cose vivono, che la mia vita per alquanti anni perseveri, spero di dire di lei quello che mai non fu detto d'alcuna.

E poi piaccia a Colui, che'è sire della cortesia, che la mia anima se ne possa gire a vedere la gloria della sua donna, cioè di quella benedetta Beatrice, che gloriosamente mira nella faccia di Colui, *qui est per omnia sæcula benedictus*.

English Translations

II

Nine times already since my birth had the heaven of light returned almost to one and the same point in relation to its own proper revolution, when the glorious lady of my mind first appeared to mine eyes, who was called Beatrice by many that knew not what they were calling her.

She already had been so long in this life that, in her time, the heaven of the stars had moved one twelfth part of a degree towards the east; so that almost from the beginning of her ninth year she appeared to me and I beheld her almost at the end of my ninth. She appeared to me clothed in the most noble hue, a subdued and modest crimson, cinctured and adorned after the fashion that was becoming to her most tender age. At that point I verily declare that the vital spirit which dwells in the most secret chamber of the heart began to tremble so mightily that it was horribly apparent in the least of my pulses, and trembling, it said these words: *Here is a god stronger than I, who shall come to rule over me.*

At that moment, the animal spirit, which dwells in the high chamber to which all the spirits of sense carry their perceptions, began to marvel much, and speaking especially to the spirits of sight said these words: *Now your beatitude has appeared.*

III

...this wondrous lady appeared to me clothed in hue of purest
white in the midst of two gentle ladies who were of fuller age;
and passing by the way she turned her eyes towards that part
where I was right fearful; and of her ineffable courtesy which
now is rewarded in the greater world, gave me a salutation of
such virtue, that methought I beheld the uttermost bounds of
blessedness.

The hour when her most sweet salutation reached me was
assuredly the ninth of that day: and in as much as that was the
first time that her words set forth to come to mine ears, such
sweetness possessed me that as one drunken I departed from all
people and withdrew to the solitude of a chamber of mine and
set me a-thinking of this most courteous one.

And as I thought of her, a gentle sleep fell upon me wherein a
wondrous vision appeared to me: for me-thought I saw in my
chamber a cloud of the hue of flame, within which I discerned
the figure of a lord, of fearful aspect to one who should look on
him. And he seemed to me of such gladness as to himself that a
wondrous thing it was; and in his words he said many things
which I understood not save a few, among which I understood
these: *Ego dominus tuus*. In his arms methought I saw one
sleeping, naked, save that she seemed to me wrapped lightly in a
crimson drapery; whom, gazing at very intently, I knew to be the
lady of the salutation, who the day before had deigned to salute
me. And in one of his hands methought he held a thing that was
all aflame; and methought he said to me these words: 'Behold
your heart'. And when he had tarried awhile, methought awoke
her who slept and so wrought he by his art that he made her eat
of that thing that was aflame in his hand, whereof she ate afeared.
Thereafter, short time he abode ere his gladness was changed to

bitterest weeping: and thus weeping he gathered this lady up in his arms and with her methought he went away heavenward: whereat I sustained so great anguish that my feeble little sleep could not endure, but broke and I was awake. And straightaway I began to ponder and found that the hour in which this vision had appeared to me had been the fourth hour of the night: so that it manifestly appears that it was the first of the last nine hours of the night.

[...]

To every captive soul and gentle heart, into whose presence come the present rhymes, that they may write me back their opinion – Greeting in their lord, to wit, Love.

Already nigh a third of the hours of the time that every star is bright to us, had passed, when suddenly Love appeared to me, the memory of whose being makes me shudder.

Gladsome Love seemed to me, holding my heart in his hand, and in his arms he had my lady, wrapped in a drapery and sleeping.

Then he awakened her and of this flaming heart, she, fearful, did humbly eat: afterwards I beheld him go his way a-weeping.

XIII

All my thoughts speak of love and have in them such great diversity, that one makes me desire his power: another argues his influence madness:

Another with hope brings my joy: another makes me weep many a time; and they only accord in craving pity, trembling at the fear that is in my heart.

Wherefore I know not from which to draw my argument, and I would speak, yet know not what to say: Thus I find me in amorous bewilderment.

And if I would make accord with all, it behoves me to call on my enemy, my lady Pity, that she defied me.

XV

If I lost not my faculties and were free so that I could answer, I would say to her that as soon as I image forth her wondrous beauty, so soon a desire possesses me to behold her, which is of such power that it slays and destroys in my memory all that could rise up against it; and therefore my past sufferings do not restrain me from seeking the sight of her. Wherefore moved by such thoughts I proposed to say certain words, wherein making my excuse unto her against such reproof I should set forth also what happened to me when near her; and I composed this sonnet:

That which befalls me, is effaced from memory when I set forth to behold you, beauteous joy, and when I am near to you I hear Love say: 'Flee, if to perish be irksome to you.'

My countenance shows the hue of my heart, which, fainting, seeks support, and with the great trembling inebriate, methinks the very stones cry out: 'Die, die.'

He who then beholds me, commits sin if he comfort not the affrighted soul by showing at least that he grieves for me

because of the pity which your mocking slays, and which is begotten of the deathly hue of eyes that desire their death.

XVI

Oft-times there comes to my memory the dark condition that Love lays on me; and pity thereof touches me, so that oft I say: 'Ah me! befalls it thus to anyone?'

For Love assails me suddenly, so that life well-night forsakes me: one spirit alone escapes alive within me and that remains, for that of you it speaks.

Then do I spur me, for fain would I aid me; and thus pallid and void of all power, I come to behold you, thinking to be made whole.

And if I lift mine eyes to gaze, a quaking begins in my heart that makes the soul to part from my pulses.

XIX

Ladies, that have intelligence of love, I would speak with you of
my lady; not because I think to exhaust her praises, but to
discourse for easement of my mind. I say, that pondering on her
worth, Love makes himself so sweetly felt within me that had I
then not lost all my daring, I should enamour folk by my speech.
And I will not speak so exaltedly that I should faint through fear;
but lightly will I touch on her gentle state in respect of her,
amorous dames and damsels, with you, for it's not a thing
whereof to speak to others.

An angel cries in the divine intelligence and says: 'Lord, in the
world a marvel is displayed in act, emanating from a soul that
shines as far as here on high. Heaven, that has none other lack
than to possess her, craves her of its Lord and every saint cries for
the grace. Pity alone defends our cause; for God speaks,
intending my lady: Beloved mine, now suffer in peace that your
hope be, so long as it pleases me, there, where is one who looks
for to lose her and who in Hell shall say to the damned: 'I have
beheld the hope of the blessed.'

My lady is desired in high heaven; now would I make you to know of her virtue. I say: whoso would seem a gentle lady let go with her; for when she passes by the way, Love casts a chill into base hearts whereby every thought of theirs is frozen and perishes. And whoso should endure to stay and behold her, would become a noble thing or else would die; and when she finds one worthy to behold her, he proves her virtue; for this befalls him, that she gives him salutation and makes him so humble he forgets every offence. Also has God given her superior grace, that whoso has spoken with her cannot end ill.

Of her says Love: 'How can a mortal thing so lovely be and pure?' Then gazes he at her, and within himself doth swear that God intends to make in her what never yet was. Suffused is she with hue as of pearls, such as beseems a lady to have, not beyond measure: she is the utmost that Nature can create of goodness: by her ensample beauty is proved. From her eyes, whereso she turns them, issue flaming spirits of Love that smite the eyes of him who then doth look on them and pierce so, that each one touches the heart. You see Love painted on her lips where none can gaze on her steadfastly.

Canzone, I know that you shall fare speaking with many ladies after I have sped you: now I admonish you, for that I have raised you up to be a daughter of Love young and guileless, that where you come you say beseechingly: 'Teach me to fare, for I am sent to her with those praises I am adorned.' And if you would not go like a vain thing, tarry not where base folk be. Contrive, if you can, to be revealed only to courteous woman or man, who shall bring you by the speedier way. There with her shall you find Love; commend me to him as is your duty.

XX

Love and a gentle heart are one same thing, even as the poet teaches in his rhymes; and one without the other dare no more exist than a rational soul apart from reason.

Nature makes them when in amorous mood, Love for lord, the heart for his dwelling-place, wherein slumbering he reposes, it may be for brief, it may be for long season.

Beauty appears in wise lady then, which is so pleasing to the eyes that within the heart a desire is born for the pleasing thing.

And some whiles it so long endures therein that it makes the spirit of love to awaken: and the like does man of worth in woman.

XXIII

While I was pondering on my frail life and beheld its length how brief it is, Love wept in my heart where he abides; whereat my soul was so bewildered, that sighing I said in thought: 'Truly it shall come to pass that my lady shall die.' Then did bewilderment so great seize me, that I closed mine eyes, basely weighed down, and so confounded were my spirits that each went forth a-wandering. And then, as I dreamed, bereft of sense and of truth, agonized faces of women appeared to me who said: 'Thou too shalt die, shalt die.'

Then saw I dread things many, in the vain vision on which I entered; and methought I was in a strange place and beheld dishevelled women going by the way, one a-weeping, another uttering lamentations that shot forth fiery shafts of grief. Then methought I beheld little by little the sun grow troubled, the stars appear, and him and them weep, birds flying in the air fall and the earth quake; and a man appeared to me pallid and faint, saying: 'What doest thou? Know you not the news? Dead is your lady that was so fair.'

Mine eyes I lifted wet with tears, and beheld (as it were a shower of manna) angels ascending heavenward and a cloudlet had they before them, following which all did shout 'Hosana' and if aught else they had said I would tell it you. Then said Love: 'No more I hide from you; come and behold our lady lying dead.' The false vision led me to behold my lady dead, and when I had perceived her I saw that ladies were covering her with a veil, and with her was humility so true that methought she said: 'I am in peace.'

XXVI

This most gentle lady of whom the preceding words were spoken came to such favour among folk, that when she passed by the way people ran to behold her, wherefore wondrous joy possessed me thereat. And when she was near to anyone, modesty so great possessed his heart that he dared not lift his eyes nor respond to her salutations; and of this many even from experienced could bear witness for me, to him who should not believe it. She, crowned and clad in humility went her way, showing no pride at what she saw and heard. Said many said after she had passed: 'This is no woman, rather is she one of the fairest angels of heaven.' And others said: 'This is a marvel and blessed be the Lord who knows how to work so wondrously.' I say that she showed herself so gentle and so filled with all winsomeness, that they who gazed upon her, felt within them a pleasant and modest sweetness, such that none could tell it again, nor was any who could look upon her without being first constrained to sigh. These and more wondrous things proceeded from her by her power. Wherefore, pondering on this, and desiring to resume the manner of her praise, I purposed to say words in which I should make some of her wondrous and excellent effects understood, in order that not only those who could behold her with their bodily senses but that others should know of her as much as words can convey to the understanding. Then I composed this sonnet:

So gentle and so modest my lady seems when she salutes others, that every tongue grows tremblingly dumb, and eyes dare not to look on her.

She goes her way, hearing her praises, benignly clothed in

humility, and seems to be a thing come from heaven to earth, to show forth a miracle.

Herself she shows so winsome to him who gazes on her, that through his eyes she gives a sweetness to his heart, such that he who proves it not, cannot understand it.

And it seems that from her countenance a spirit moves, gentle and filled with love, that goes saying to the soul: sigh.

XXXI

Sorrowing for pity of my heart, mine eyes have suffered such pain of weeping that now they lie vanquished. Now if I would ease my sorrow that little by little brings me unto death, it behoves me to speak uttering lamentations. And because I remember that I spoke of my lady, while she lived, gentle ladies, willingly with you, I would not speak of her to others, save to a gentle heart that in woman may be. And weeping, will tell of her, since she has passed straightaway to heaven and hath left Love with me sorrowing.

[...]

Sighs give me great anguish, when in my heavy memory, thought recalls to me her who has cleft my heart, and oft-times thinking of death, there comes upon me a desire so sweet that it changes the hue of my countenance. When the vision holds me right steadfastly, pain so great seizes me on every side that I return to myself through the sorrow I feel, and so changed become that shame sunders me from all people. Then weeping, I call alone on Beatrice in my lamentation, and say: 'Now are you dead!' And while I call on her, am comforted.

XXXVII

I came to such pass by the sight of this lady that mine eyes began to delight over much in beholding her, wherefore many times I was angry in my heart and held me therefore exceeding base; and many times did I curse the inconstancy of mine eyes and said to them in my thoughts: 'Come, ye were wont to make weep such as beheld your grievous state, and now it seems that you would forget it because of this lady who gazes at you, and gazes not at you save in so far as she is weighed down for the glorious lady for whom you were wont to weep; but, what you can, do; for I will recall her to you very often, accursed eyes: since never save after death ought your tears to be stayed. And when I had thus said within myself to mine eyes, lo, sighs most heavy and choking assailed me. And in order that this conflict which I had within me should not remain known to the wretch only who suffered it, I purposed to make a sonnet and to comprehend in it this dreadful condition...

XLI

Beyond the sphere, that circles widest, passes the sigh that issues from my heart; a new faculty that weeping Love implants in it, draws it ever upwards.

When it has reached there whereto it yearns, it beholds a lady, that receives honour and shines so, that for her splendour the pilgrim spirit gazes on her.

It beholds her such, when it retells it me, I understand it not, so subtly it speaks to the sorrowing heart that makes it to speak.

I know that it speaks of that gentle lady, for oft it recalls Beatrice, so that I understand it well, dear ladies mine.

XLII

After this sonnet there appeared to me a wondrous vision, wherein I beheld things that made me determine to speak no more of this blessed one until such time as I could treat of her more worthily. And to attain to this I study all I may, even as she truly knows. So that if it be the pleasure of him, by whom all things live, that in my life persevere for some few years, I hope to write of her what has never been written of any woman.

And then may it please him who is the Lord of grace, that my soul may have leave to go and behold the glory of its lady, to wit, of that blessed Beatrice who gazes in glory on the face of him, *who is through all ages blessed.*

Illustrations

Images of Dante Alighieri, and art based on Dante's work.

Andrea del Castagno, Dante Alighieri, 1450,
Uffizi Gallery, Florence

Luca Signorelli, Dante Alighieri, fresco in Orvieto Cathedral

Giorgio Vasari, Six Tuscan Poets, 1544, Minneapolis

Elisabeth Sonrel, Scenes From Dante Alighieri's Vita Nuova

Sandro Botticelli, The Map of Hell, 1480-90, Vatican

Antonio Cotti, Dante In Verona, 1879, Lyon

Eugène Delacroix, The Barque of Dante,
1822, Louvre

Eugene-Auguste-Francois Deully, Dante and Virgil in Hell, 1897

Enrico Pazzi, Dant Alighieri, 1875, Santa Croce

Rafael Flores, Dante and Virgil Visiting the Inferno,
1855, Mexico City

Andrea Pierini, Dante alla corte di Guido Novello,
1855, Florence

Dante Gabriel Rossetti, Dante's Dream At the Time of the Death
of Beatrice, 1871, Walker Art Gallery

Dante Gabriel Rossetti, Beata Beatrix, 1864-70, Tate Britain

Marie Spartall Stillman, Beatrice, 1915

John William Waterhouse, Dante and Matilda, 1915,
Dahesh Museum of Art

A NOTE ON DANTE'S *VITA NUOVA*

Dante Alighieri's *Vita Nuova* is his 'Book of Memory', the poetic account of his love for Beatrice Portinari. The *Vita Nuova* or *New Life* draws on (and is part of) the *dolce stil novo,* the 'sweet new style' of poets such as Guido Cavalcanti, Guido Guinicelli, Cino da Pistoia and other *stilnovisti.* Dante was an admirer of courtly love poetry (he praised Arnaut Daniel in the *Divina Commedia*).[1] Among the influences on the *Vita Nuova* are, of course, the Bible (in particular the Psalms, the *Song of Songs*, Jeremiah's *Lamentations* and Christ's Passion); other influences, apart from Classical thinkers, are Aelred of Rievaulx's *De spirituali amicitia* and Peter of Blois's *Deamicitia christiana* (Anderson, 136). Classical and earlier writers whom Dante read included Cicero (*De amicitia*) and Boethius (*De consolatione*). The *Vita Nuova*, though, stands on its own in mediæval literature. There is nothing else quite like it. Whereas Abelard produced a 'passionate self-exculpation' and Boethius was facing death, Dante wrote a creative autobiography, a record of his emotional and creative life up until the year 1294. it was inevitable, it seems, that women should be so etherealized they become angels. We see this angelization in poems such as Cavalcanti's "Veggio negli occhi", where the woman dazzles the narrator.[2] In Guinicelli's *canzone* "A cor gentil" the poet tells God that the *donna*: '[t]enne d'angel sembianza | Che fosse del Tuo regno' ('she was like an angel who was of your kingdom') (O'Donoghue, 1982, 264-5). In poem 19 of *Vita Nuova*, Dante writes: 'Madonna è disïata in sommo cielo' ('My lady is desired in heaven on high', O'Donoghue, 286-7). In the *canzone* "Amor che ne la mente mi ragiona", also from *Vita Nuova*, Dante says that 'divine power descends upon her as it does onto an angel that sees it' (O'Donoghue, 295). The angelic women of the *stilnovisti* – Giovanna, Selvaggia, Beatrice – are amazingly radiant, they make people gasp when they walk by; their eyes can kill; they outshine the sun; they are practically superhuman.

The personages in the *Vita Nuova* include the poet, his friends, various ladies, Beatrice, God and the Lord of Love, who is not always identical with God. If the *New Life* were a courtly love scenario, the poet would be content with loving the lady. However, the Dante-poet, like the Petrarch-poet, is not satisfied to stop there.[3] There must be something more. That 'something' is the divine. At the end of Petrarch's *Canzoniere*, above and beyond Laura is the Virgin Mary; beyond Beatrice in the *Vita Nuova* (and in the *Divina Commedia*) is God. The mediæval monk or saint would have looked for God; the troubadour to Beatrice; Dante is somewhere between the two. He is never wholly convincing (as with Petrarch) that he is going to exalt divine love higher than earthly love. Similarly, the Dante-poet's view of the Lord of Love is not of a wholly divine being (God), but someone who can intercede in human (love) affairs.

Dante first met Beatrice at a party given by her father Folco Portinari, the Florentine banker, on Mayday, 1274. He was nearly nine; she was nearly eight. She was wearing a red dress, and was known as Bice, a shortened form of Beatrice. The *Vita Nuova* relates the Dante-poet's experience of Beatrice in 25 sonnets, one *ballata*, three *canzoni* and two incomplete *canzoni* consisting of one stanza and two stanzas in length. The *Vita Nuova* was the first book to link together poems and a prose commentary of an autobiographical and critical nature. The mixture of prose and poetry was known in mediæval times as a *prosimetrum* narrative. In the first chapters of the *New Life* Dante describes his first sightings of Beatrice.[4] The poetic style with which Dante first eulogizes Beatrice is ornate and involved - some would say pompous. Once one becomes used to Dante's sometimes circumluitous lyrical style in his prose (and his poetry), one recognizes the force of his experience. It is one of the great meetings of young lovers in the history of Western art.

Notice how Dante moves swiftly from the radiance of the beloved to a record of her effect upon him, upon his trembling heart. What interests him is not so much her as her ability to make him feel. The next meeting is nine years later, at the ninth hour. The significance of the number nine for Dante has been remarked upon by critics for hundreds of years. The number is the symbol of his love for Beatrice, a symbolic expression of his love experience. It is the number of his desire: it keeps cropping up partly because he wants to see it everywhere, because he wants to see his beloved everywhere (and his own loving projected outwards). The number nine becomes the symbolic basis of his love of Beatrice. It is the number of that all important event, Beatrice's death. She died in the 9th decade of the 13th century. In the Arabian calendar, she died in the first hour of the ninth day of the month; in the Syrian reckoning, she died in the 9th month of the year. At her birth, the poet says, the nine heavens of spheres were in perfect harmony. Another point the poet makes is that Beatrice is the number nine in herself, symbolically, as the poet says: he relates three squared (= 9) to the Trinity: 'since three is the maker by itself of nine, and the Maker by Itself of miracles is three, that is, Father and Son and Holy Ghost, which are three and one, this lady was accompanied by this number nine in order to signify that she was a nine, that is, a miracle, whose root, that is, of the miracle, is only the

75

marvellous Trinity (*Vita Nuova*, XXIX, 61; hereafter as VN). Significantly, the poet admits after this convoluted exegesis, that other interpretations may be possible, 'but this is the one that I see and that pleases me the most.'

The number three is important too in the Vita *Nuova*. Beatrice's death is seen by the Dante-poet as the central panel in a poetic triptych. The central part of the triptych of the *Vita Nuova* is taken up by the *canzone* "Donna pietosa". This symbolic pattern of the number three can be broken up into patterns of nine: setting aside the 1st and last poems as an introduction and epilogue, the rest of the poems constitute a pattern of 1, 9, I, 4-II-4, III, 9, 1.). The Roman numerals signify the three main *canzoni*, the other poems and sonnets are in Arabic numbers. Another way of depicting the pattern of three and nine is thus: 1, 9, 1, 9, 1, 9, 1. With Beatrice's death as the central fact of the Vita *Nuova*, a symmetrical pattern is disclosed, with Beatrice before her death being mirrored in the latter part of the sequence by Beatrice in glory as the *donna angelicata*. Other incidents are mirrored: the women of the screen and the *donna gentile*, for example, or Love as the pilgrim in the poem "Cavalcando l'altr'ier" and the pilgrim in "Deh peregrini". The *canzone* "Donne ch'avete" is reflected by "Li occhi dolenti". The death of Beatrice is mirrored by the death of her father.

The mere sight of Beatrice is enough to overcome the Dante-poet with ecstasy. He has to retire, in order to make sense of his intoxication. And of course he does so by writing about it, which is what poets have done from the age of Sappho and Homer onwards. First comes the ecstasy of love, but just as important is the writing about it. Out of this experience of love and the dream of the heart-red dress-fire-Love-Beatrice motifs it inaugurates comes the first sonnet of the *Vita Nuova*, "A ciascun'alma presa e gentil core". Dante makes the connections very clear between experience, dream and poetry. The experience becomes embroiled in the unconscious and dreaming: to make sense of all this is the poetry. The poetry becomes conscious analysis of

76

experience. It is literally 'dreamwork', to use the Freudian term. In chapter III of his *Vita Nuova*, then, Dante outlines the psychoanalytic interpretation of making art. Dante describes in easily recognisable and 'modern' terms the trajectory of creation from experience to dream to art.

The effect of the beloved's greeting upon the Dante-poet is so extraordinary that he is rendered incapable of will and independent action. He gives himself up (or is given up by forces outside himself) to love (or the Lord of Love) and the *donna*. The experience of love itself (embodied in the figure of the Lord of Love) is so overwhelming that the Dante-poet is forced to endure 'unbearable bliss', and his body becomes controlled by the Lord of Love. In one of Dante's typically extreme images, his body is 'quasi per soperchio di dolcezza divenia tale' ('possessed with an excess of sweetness', VN, 18).

The violence of Dante's poetry of love is very apparent: though intensely lyrical, his poetry is not wimpy and 'gentle' (though it does celebrate tenderness). Rather, Dante employs the full force of the mediæval concept of love: as an arrow of love fired by Venus's helper, Cupid, which literally enters the eye and thence the heart. In the *Vita Nuova canzone* "Amor che ne la mente mi ragiona", Dante's persona speaks of Beatrice's beauty as pouring down 'flames of fire' which 'smash like a thunderbolt the inborn evils that make someone base' (O'Donoghue, 297). The glance of the beloved is extremely powerful, so that the poet's soul quivers when she looks at him. In the poem "Al poco giorno e al gran cerchio d'ombra" the narrator says Beatrice's beauty has 'more force than rock', and he can never escape from her look (O'Donoghue, 291).

Beatrice was the pretext for Dante's explorations of love poetry and religious imagery. Rather than the 'real' woman herself, the poetic exaltation of her is one of the driving forces behind the *Divina Commedia*. The subject of the *Vita Nuova*, similarly, is not so much Beatrice as Dante's lyrical evocation of her.[5] Beatrice is the excuse for indulgent poeticizing, as if Dante or any poet needs an excuse. But invoking an idealized lady like Beatrice, or the names of Christ and the Virgin Mary, elevates the poetic enterprise. The self-reflectivity of Dante's poetry is 'modern', it partakes of a modernist *mise-en-abyme*, where (love) poetry is worked with a system of mirrors. One keeps returning to motifs and metaphors of light and mirrors because that is how Dante keeps imagining things. In the *Paradiso*, for example, there is that elaborate 'scientific' set-up of mirrors (II. 94-105). Dante's poetry is full of mirrors – of being able to see in mirrors, or through veils, or smoke, or clouds; to see clearly; or having obscured vision; or going blind; or not being able to look upon something incredibly beautiful (Beatrice, the Virgin and God).

In the *Vita Nuova*, though the beloved remains untouchable, Dante's narrator's love of Beatrice has an erotic element. The sheer force of his adulation eroticizes their relationship. He trembles violently when he sees her, and thinks she is the cause of it, whereas she is merely the trigger. Hardly any words are exchanged – and the beloved often hardly even gives him a glance. Dante's is the supreme expression of the troubadours' 'loving from afar', *amor lonh*: he sustains it over a whole sequence of poems the *Vita Nuova*). There are many moments in the *Divine Comedy, Convivio* and *Vita Nuova* which suggest that the Dante-Beatrice affair was 'real'. Well, their love was 'real' enough for him. Or at least real enough for him to portray himself as suffering for love in many *canzoni* and commentaries.[6] Much of the *Vita Nuova* has the intensity and unreality of a dream: the force of Dante's poetic vision gives events a bright, hallucinatory edge. There is also the dream in the *Vita Nuova*, with its fervent Catholic imagery: the fire, the red dress, the heart, the burning sensations. It is a highly erotic dream – no need to refer to Freud to see that. The poet has just returned to his rooms after beholding the *bella donna* in the street after a 9-year gap.

The erotic quality of the red dress dream would obvious to anyone familiar with the sensuality of Arthurian romance, vernacular courtly poetry, commentaries on Classic myths, even

Catholic mysticism, such as St Bernard's sermons or Hildegaard of Bingen's writings. In the dream the lovelorn poet fantasizes about Beatrice: she is naked under a 'crimson cloth'. The dream, as fantastical as the most 'visionary' parts of the *Divine Comedy*, ends with an act of oral eroticism: Love gives Dante's 'burning heart' to Beatrice, who eats it. Historical commentators might note that Beatrice's red dress relates to Christ's Passion and the notion of sacrifice and faith. Freudian critics might discuss the imagery of castration and self-denial. Few commentators have noted the strong menstrual discourse in Dante's dream: the crimson dress (VN, 4) is symbolic of menstruation and of blood rites.

After chapter three, with its first sonnet and dream of Beatrice in the red cloth, Dante's narrator continues to develop his sense of selfhood. For example, at the end of chapter three, Dante's poet mentions that he sent his first sonnet to a friend (Cavalcanti). A sense of shame is also apparent: '[t]he true interpretation of the dream I described was not perceived by anyone then, but now it is very clear to even the least sophisticated' he admits (VN, 7) That is, a dream of a naked lover clad in a loose crimson cloth is really about good old-fashioned sexual lust.

The sexual dimension of the Dante-poet's love for Beatrice is never lost, even when she is angelicized as the *donna angelicata*. For example, in his explication of the key *canzone* "Donna ch'avete", the Dante-poet says he is speaking of the 'magnificence of her soul', which is quite right. But he also says he is describing 'particular parts of her body'. The eyes, first and foremost, as always in the scopophilic art of courtly love poetry, but also, he says, 'nella seconda dico ella bocca la quale è fine d'Amore' ('secondly I speak of her mouth, which is the supreme desire of my love', VN, 38). Lest any reader should determine that the Dante-poet is thinking sinful thoughts about his glorious madonna, he goes on to explain how the *donna*'s greeting comes out of her mouth, so her mouth must be one of his objects of adoration. The Dante-poet could have said 'her voice', or 'the words she spoke', instead of 'her mouth'. In speaking of her mouth, the Dante-poet eroticizes the beloved, even though he claims he is not doing so. In part XVI, the Dante-poet admits he is in lust as well as in love with Beatrice.

The *Vita Nuova* is successful (and still read) partly because it is infused with such a depth and intensity of (erotic) desire. Again and again the Dante-poet admits that he cannot think of anything else except Beatrice (or, more accurately, his love for her). The Dante-poet cannot see anything but Beatrice. His image of her (rather than the woman herself) is what keeps haunting him, preventing him from seeing anything else. Her ghost dominates him, in true Jungian *anima* fashion. 'Cosi mi trovo in amorosa erranza' ('thus do I wander in a maze of Love') moans the Dante-poet in 'Sonnetto Sesto' (part XIII, VN, 24). The Dante-poet in love becomes an image of love itself. As he experiences love, he becomes an image of love. If the reader wants to know what love is like, he says in part eleven, just look 'at my trembling eyes' (VN, 18).

Dante's poet's sense of selfhood is very apparent from the beginning of the *New Life* onwards: at the end of chapter III, the poet mentions that he is starting to circulate his sonnets. In the short chapter four, Dante's poet starts to see himself and his new love reflected in the eyes and admiration of his friends and peers. His friends, he says, became concerned about his listlessness and frailty. A certain smugness is found in the newly-in-love poet, as he smiles and says nothing to people's questions of '[f]or whom has Love so undone you?' (VN, 8)

Beatrice seems unaware of the immense effect she has upon the hapless poet. He, meanwhile, is at the mercy of the god of Love, and the Goddess, Beatrice. Distance soon rewrites their relationship: soon he is viewing Beatrice from a distance, and it is thence, the *memory* of her that fires him up, as with Petrarch's remembrance of Laura (VN, 29). Dante calls his series of prose and poems a 'book of memory'. As Dante's narrator becomes a slave to Love ('[s]i langamente m' ha tenuto Amore', 'so long a time has Love kept me a slave', 59), Beatrice moves ever further into the distance. The poet can only muse on her from afar: it is the classic scenario of courtly *amor lonh*. Rather than the hoped-for pattern of sensual touches and the murmured exchanges of lovers, the woebegone narrator hovers around her, sighing dolefully. He wallows in his holy martyrdom of love. He stresses the honesty and nobility of his loving and his undertaking of adoring the blessed woman. Yet he remains curiously ineffectual, impotent to act. After he's seen her, he scurries back to his rooms and writes a poem about it. The experiene of love thus needs the poem to make it 'real': writing is necessary to make the poet feel alive, feel as if he's really living through his hell of love. The *Vita Nuova* is a literary record as much as an emotional one. With *il dolce stil novo*, art triumphs over raw experience: it's all very well living, but it's no good unless life can be refashioned into art. This is the modern æsthetic stance, found in André Gide, Lawrence Durrell, Rainer Maria Rilke, Marcel Proust and James Joyce. Dante's self-awareness is thus distinctly 'modern', and the Trecento and the late Middle Ages can be seen, in one way, as the birth of the early 'modern' world. Of course, one can provide any date for the 'birth' of the modern age: some critics look back to Nietzsche, Freud and Marx, others go back further, to Baudelaire, or the Romantics, or the French Revolution, or to the Age of Enlightenment, or the Renaissance, or the mediæval world, or even to ancient Greece, with its creation of Christian and democratic politics. In Dante and the *stilnovisti*, though, we see so clearly that acute self-consciousness which is so 'modern', a self-reflexivity that is so much a part of modern society (think of the navel-gazing literary theorists, or the self-regarding media stars). The *dolce stil novo* was art about art, an æstheticization of literary æsthetics. In the *Vita Nuova* the woman, the love-relationship, the nuances of sensuality and circumstance are transcended in favour of a poetry that exalts the art of poetry, memory and refinement (and the poet himself).

In the *dolce stil novo*, love is on the point of death; that is, the beloved is on the point of passing away, because she is so beautiful, and the lover's joy is so intense it seems it will kill him. Like the portrayal of the orgasm in later European writers such as the Marquis de Sade, Charles Baudelaire and Georges Bataille, love in *dolce stil novo* poetry is so incredible that it resembles the exquisite passing away into death or Heaven. The goal, in *dolce stil novo* poetry, was always to get to Heaven. It was as if earthly love could never be as great or as important as divine love. Earthly love was the model merely, the precursor of a sublime union in Heaven. However great earthly love was, it was always supereded by heavenly love. Whatever joys the *stilnovisti* lovers experienced on Earth, they would be transcended when they reached Heaven (if they were allowed to reach Heaven). Other cultures and viewpoints have seen earthly love as divine in itself, not needing the blessing or presence of God or heaven to make it sacred. The notions of 'heavenly' and 'earthly' love are, anyway, metaphors - for states of mind, for philosophies, for experiences. Earthly love, at its best - the orgasmic, intimate exchange between lovers - was *already* divine, holy, sacred, heavenly. This is the view of the post-Renaissance world, which does not need God or religion to crown love. In the mediæval world, however, the individual must always defer to God, earthly love to divine love.

Some critics have complained that Beatrice is a fuzzy, vague persona: but this is so that Dante the poet can transform her into an angel. The portrait of Dante's beloved must remain hazy: if he had drawn her with all her 'real', physical idiosyncrasies - a hairy top lip, a tick in the eye, broken, chapped skin, an uneven hairline - with all her 'imperfections', Beatrice could not have become an angel. Beatrice is more than an angel, too. Angels are sparks of light, splinters of the Divine Light (God), beings (in the Rilkean model) of speed and violence who exist somewhere between Here and There, between Then and Now, Heaven and Earth. Beatrice in the *Divine Comedy* becomes a special kind of guide who can traverse the whole of Heaven: she is more than the *donna angeliata*. Beatrice leaves Earth and ascends to heaven to become one of the guides on the magical mystery tour of the *Divina Commedia*.

One of the key poems in the *Vita Nuova* is in chapter XIX, 'Ladies, refined' ('Donna, ch'avete'). In this *canzone* one finds all the tenets and desires associated with Dante and the *stilnovisti*. Indeed, the very first line brings together some of the key concepts of the *dolce stil nuovo*: ladies, sensitivity and refinement, and love (also the Lord of Love). In line 4, the poet admits that 'talking...may ease my mind': in this case, he means writing: the self-assuagement that writing may bring. In line 5, the Dante-poet begins to exalt his lady: and his lyrical exaltation naturally flows back to his own self: 'her worthiness' makes 'a love so sweet' 'felt in me' (VN, 35). It is, thus, just as much his own ability to absorb her worthiness, as well as her worthiness in itself, that is important to the poet. The lady is eminently worthy, but somehow this worthiness rubs off onto the Dante-poet. In the next few lines, the poet discusses how he is going to sing of Beatrice: how his too-lofty tone may make the song fail; sensitivity in love is equated with sensitivity in art. Good loving equals good poetry; or the best of love demands the best of poetry. A woman as worthy as Beatrice and the wonder of the love between them (at least from the poet's point of view) demands excellent poetry. The (self-imposed) demand the woman, Love and their love makes, then, is for great, beautifully-crafted poetry. This is how the Dantean (and troubadour) poet interprets his love relationship with the beloved woman. Her mere existence demands great lyrical flights: simply by being alive she requires that great poetry be written about her. The Dante/ *stilnovisti* poet personifies these (conflicting) demands of love, life and art in the person of Love, the Lord of Love. The ambiguities and confusions of courtly and *dolce stil novo* poetry is embodied in the figure of Love, who is and is not identified with God, who is sometimes the poet's projections, or the poet's desire. *Canzone* XIX of the *Vita Nuova* also contains some deliciously far-fetched conceits. For example, the poet goes swiftly to the centre of the universe (the mind of God) and has an angel announce that on earth there is a 'living miracle' (Beatrice) whose light is so radiant it reaches even Heaven. Further: Heaven is not complete ('lacks its full perfection') because it lacks Beatrice's radiance. It is a bombastic conceit, that Heaven is not quite perfect without Beatrice, that all the saints are begging God to bring her there. The poet then has God speaking warmly of himself – this is the ultimate in self-glorification: writing a poem in which God blesses the lowly poet. Instead of reflecting his glory in the beloved woman, or in another poet or his fellow peers, or in a saint, or even in the Virgin Mary, the Dante-poet has himself enlarged by God's own vision and talk (VN, 36).

To demonstrate just how fabulous his *donna* is, Dante's poet claims that she is 'desired in highest heaven' (VN, 36). Later, in the *Commedia*, the Dante-pilgrim conjures up a system of metaphoric mirrors and reflections, so that the majesty of God is reflected first onto Beatrice, thereby mythicizing her, and thence (inevitably) onto the poet himself. Speaking of God in noble, haughty (yet also humble) tones automatically ennobles the speaking subject: writing poetry becomes a system of meta-phorical mirrors, in which the power of the Divine Light is bounced around, eventually ending up reflected onto the poet-pilgrim's own personality.[7] Dante's *selva oscura* or dark forest is associated, as in fairy tales, with (Christian) sin, alienation from God and error. The poet-pilgrim in the *selva oscura* is cut off from God, the 'straight way' is lost, and the task of the *Comedy* is to reach the Divine Light. The hero/ heroine/ subject of both the *Vita Nuova* and the *Divina Commedia* is not God, nor the Lord of Love, nor Beatrice, nor the Virgin Mary, but the Dante-poet himself and his amazing text.

Remnants of the Dante cult can still be encountered in Florence. In one of the shady mediæval alleys, for example, one can visit Dante's house. Casa Dante is a not exceptional town house, but the rooms are cool and spacious. Here, one is supposed to contemplate, Dante *actually lived.* This house in a Florentine side street is more impressive than being in, say, Shakespeare's birthplace, or his town house of New Place in Stratford. Somehow Dante's House in Florence takes one back much further than Shakespeare's time, which does not seem *that* far off. In Dante's House, though, there is a connection to something far older; not a Renaissance world, but a mediæval world: a world with a philosophy not centred, as in the Renaissance, on humanity, but on God and Christianity. There is a massive difference: Renaissance philosophy is essentially our philosophy: human-centred, humanist, liberal, polymath. The mediæval world of Dante, which one can sense in those dark Florentine backstreets, is altogether older, tougher, more crude perhaps, more fervent, more fearful: a link back to the Dark Ages, and to the Classical world (even though the Renaissance claimed to have a monopoly on that). Wandering out of Casa Dante, one can also see the very church where Dante saw Beatrice, Chiesa di Dante. A little sign informs one of their meeting. Here they honour *Il Giorno di Beatrice.* If it's not historically accurate, it doesn't matter. What counts is the magic of their myth, as with Heloise and Abelard, or Petrarch and Laura. Little is known of Beatrice (as with Laura and other courtly love poets' beloveds). After all, Beatrice and Laura were not *writers*, not (as far as current research suggests) ardent recorders of their daily and spiritual lives, as Dante and Petrarch were. Dante and his contemporaries could not help writing down their thoughts: thus one knows far more about Dante than Beatrice. The other problem with knowing the 'real' Beatrice is that she has become known largely through Dante's writings. She is a mediated, represented presence, a product (a figment, as Samuel Beckett would say) of Dante's texts. The sheer force of Dante's poetic texts flies above the more plodding historical accounts of the time. Dante glorified himself, and Beatrice, but Beatrice did not write herself, to counter her mediation in Dante's texts. With Dante's poetry of Beatrice on one side and the scant historical evidence of her on the other, it is no wonder that Dante's account of Beatrice should be so influential, colouring even 'objective' and dispassionate historical accounts.

NOTES

1. On Dante and the troubadours, see L.T. Topsfield. *Troubadours and Love*, Cambridge University Press, 1975; Michelanglo Picone. "La *Vita Nuova* e la tradizone poetica", *Dante Studies*, 95, 1977, "I travatori di Dante: Bertran de Born", *Studi e problemi di critica testuale*, 19, 1979, and "Giraut de Bornelh nella prospettiva di Dante", *Vox Romanica*, 39, 1980; Linda M. Paterson. *Troubadours and Eloquence*, Oxford University Press, 1975; Newman, 1968; James V. Mirollo. "In Praise of Labella mano: Aspects of Late Renaissance Lyricism", *Comparative Literature Studiesø*, 9, 1972; Ronald L. Martinez. "Dante and the Two Canons", *Comparative Literature Studies*, 32, 1955; Jack Lindsay. *Troubadours and Their World*, Frederick Muller, 1976; Moshe Lazar & Norris Lacy, eds. *The Poetics of Love in the Middle Ages: Texts and Contexts*, George Mason University Press, Fairfax, Va., 1989; Laura Kendrick. *The Game of Love: Troubadour Wordplay*, University of California Press, Los Angeles, 1988; F.R.P. Akehurst. "Words and Acts in the Troubadours", in Lazar, 1989; Peter Hainsworth *et al*, eds. *The Languages of Literature in Renaissance Italy*, Oxford University Press, 1988 and "Cavalcanti in the *Vita Nuova*", *Modern Language Review*, 83, 1988; Henry Chaytor: *The Troubadours of Dante*, Oxford University Press, 1902; Meg Bogin: *The Women Troubadours*, Paddington Press, New York, 1976; R. Boase: *The Origin and Meaning of Courtly Love*, Manchester University Press, 1977; Thomas Bergin: "Dante's Provençal Gallery",

Speculum, 40, 1965; Robert Briffault: *The Troubadours*, ed. Koons, Indiana University Press, Bloomington, 1965; A.J. Denomy: "Fin' Amors: The Pure Love of the Troubadours, Its Amorality and Possible Source", *Medieval Studies*, 7, 1945 and "*Jois* Among the Early Troubadours", *Medieval Studies*, 13, 1951; Klaus Kropfinger: "Dante e l'arte dei trovatori", in Pestalozza, 1988; Ulrich Mölk: *Trobar clus, trobar leu*, Fink, Munich, 1968; W.D. Paden: "The Troubadour's Lady", *Studies in Philology*, 72, 1975; F. Pirot: "Dante et les troubadours", *Marche romane*, 15, 1965; Maurizio Perugi: "Ill Sordello di Dante e la tradizione mediolatina dell'invettiva", *Studi danteschi*, 55, 1983.

On Dante and the troubadour Arnaut Daniel, see: Ronald L. Martinez: "Dante Embarks Arnaut", *NEMLA Italian Studies*, 15, 1991; Elio Melli: "Dante e Arnaut Daniel", *Filologia romanza*, 6, 1959; Maurizio Perugi: "Dante e Arnaut Daniel", *Studi Danteschi*, 51, 1978; Maria Picchio Simonelli: "La sestina Dantesca fra Arnaut Daniel e il Petrarca", *Dante Studies*, 91, 1973.

2. Cavalcanti, in G.R. Ceriello, *Rimatoria del dolce stil novo*, Milan 1950, 63.

3. On Dante and Petrarch, see P. Trovato. *Dante in Petrarca: Per un inventario dei dantismi nei Rerum Vulgarium Fragmente*, Florence, 1979; F. Suitner. *Petrarca e la tradizione stilnovistica*, Florence, 1977; A. Scaglione, ed. *Francis Petrarch: Six Centuries Later*, Chicago University Press, 1975; M. Santagata. *Dal sonetto al canzoniere*, Padua, 1979 and "Presenze di Dante 'comico' nel 'Canzoniere' del Petrarca", *Giornale storic della letteratura italiana*, 146, 1969; A. Moschetti. *Dell' Inspirazione dantesca nelle Rime di Francesco Petrarca,* Urbana 1894; Julius A. Molinaro, ed. *Petrarch to Pirandello*, University of Toronto Press, Toronto, 1973; Roland Greene. *Post-Petrarchism: Origins and Innovations of the Western Lyric Sequence*, Princeton University Press, Princeton, 1991; Michele Feo. "Petrarca e Dante", *Enciclopedia Dantesca*, 4, 1973; L.W. Foster. *The Icy Fire: Five Studies in European Petrarchism*, Cambridge University Press, 1969; G. Billanovich: "Tra Dante e Petrarca", *Italia medievale e*

umanistica, 8, 1965; J. Larner: *Italy in the Age of Dante and Petrarch*, London, 1980; Aldo Bernardo, ed. "Petrarch's attitude towards Dante", *Proceedings of the Modern Language Association*, 70, 1955, & A.L. Pellegrini, eds: *Dante, Petrarch, Boccaccio, Medieval and Renaissance Texts and Studies*, Binghamton, 1983

4. In a *canzone* Dante left out of the *Vita Nuova* ("E'm' increasce") he says he felt the moment of the birth of Beatrice in his soul when he was one. So powerful was Beatrice's birth in the one year-old Dante's soul he fainted. (Dante, 1967, 32).

5. Mario Marti writes that the *stilnovisti* lady is attenuated, and 'disappears into the mist of a symbol', where her few physical attributes (her sweet smile, radiant eye, golden hair) are spiritualized and reduced, 'till they become mere signs of a state of mind intoxicated by the ecstasy of contemplation'. The lady becomes the 'symbol of self-contemplation' (Marti, 1972, 159-160).

6. In *stilnovisti* writing the soul (or heart) is the site of suffering; the struggle sometimes is represented by psychomachia, or in the effects of the struggle, in weeping and signing. 'The suffering self, the object of the narration, is inarticulate, since neither tears nor sighs are verbal: the narrating self then takes these sighs and gives them a textual presence: the poem is 'the sound of a sigh' or 'is written in tears'' (Spiller, 1992, 42).

7. The *Divine Comedy* moves from darkness to light: it opens with the pilgrim lost in a forest, one of the classic images of the wilderness or unconscious: '[i]n the middle of life's path | I found myself in a dark forest | where the straight way was lost' (*Inferno*, I: 1-3). In the *Divine Comedy*, the forest is not only allegorical, but theological. (Harrison, 1992, 81)

SELECT BIBLIOGRAPHY

DANTE ALIGHIERI

Le Opere di Dante Alighieri, ed. E. Moore, Oxford University Press, 1963
Vita Nuova, tr. Mark Musa, Oxford University Press, 1992
The Portable Dante, ed. Mark Musa, Penguin, 1995
Dante's Lyric Poetry, ed. K. Foster & P. Boyde, Oxford University Press, 1967
Rime della 'Vita Nuova' e della giovinezza, eds. M. Barbi & F. Maggini, Le Monnier, Florence, 1956
Dante: Literature in the Vernacular, Manchester University Press, 1981

Richard Abrams. "Illicit Pleasures: Dante Among the Sensualists", *Modern Language Notes*, 100, 1985

William Anderson. *Dante the Maker*, Hutchinson, 1980

J.A. Barber. "The Role of the Other in Dante's *Vita Nuova*", *Studies in Philology*, 78, 1981

Teodolinda Barolini. *The Undivine "Comedy", Dethroning Dante*, Princeton University Press, 1992

Thomas Bergin. *A Diversity of Dante*, Rutgers University Press, New Brunswick, 1969

—. ed. *From Time to Eternity*, Yale University Press, New Haven, 1967

Dino Bigongiari. "Dante's *Vita Nuova*" in *Essays on Dante and Medieval Culture*, Olshki, Florence, 1964

Harold Bloom, ed. *Dante*, Chelsea House, New York, 1986

Umberto Bosco, ed. *Enciclopedia dantesca*, 6 vols, Instituto dell'Enciclopedia Italiana, 1970-78

—. *Handbook to Dante Studies,* Oxford, 1950

C.M. Bowra. *Inspiration and Poetry*, Macmillan, 1955

Marina S. Brownlee *et al*, eds. *The New Medievalism*, John Hopkins University Press, Baltimore, 1991

Michael Caesar, ed. *Dante: The Critical Heritage 1314(?)-1870*, Routledge, 1989

M. Carruthers. *The Book of Memory: A Study of Memory in Medieval Culture,* Olschki, Florence, 1964

Dino Cervigni, ed. *Dante and Modern American Criticism, Annalis d'Italianistica*, 8, 1990

—. *Dante's Poetry of Dreams*, Olschki, Florence, 1986

R.J. Clements, ed. *Dante: A Collection of Critical Essays,* New Jersey, 1965

Stelio Cro. "*Vita Nuova* figura *Comoediae*: Dante tra la Villana Morte e Matelda", *Italian Culture*, 6, 1985

Antonio D'Andrea. "La struttura della *Vita Nuova*: Le divisioni delle rime", *Yearbook of Italian Studies*, 4, 1980

Margherita De Bonfils Templer. *Itinerario di Amore: Dialettica di Amore e Morte nella* Vita Nuova, University of North Carolina Studies in Romance Languages and Literatures, Chapel Hill, 1973

Domenico De Roberts, ed. *Vita Nuova*, Riccardo Ricciardi, Milan, 1980

—. *Il libro della* Vita Nuova, Sansoni, Florence, 1970

Peter Dronke. *The Medieval Lyric*, Hutchinson, 1968

Robert M. Durling & Ronald L. Martinez. *Time and the Crystal: Studies in Dante's 'Rime Petrose'*, University of California Press, Berkeley, 1990

Heather Dubrow. *Echoes of Desire: English Petrarchism and Its Counterdiscourses,* Cornell University Press, 1995

Gerda Elata-Aster. "Gathering the Leaves and Squaring the Circle: *Recording, Reading* and *Writing* in Dante's *Vita Nuova* and *Divina Commedia*", *Italian Quarterly*, 24, 92, 1983

J.B. Fletcher. *Dante*, Notre Dame University Press, 1965

-"The True Meaning of Dante's Vita Nuova", *Romanic Review*, 11, 1920

Kenhelm Foster. "The Mind in Love: Dante's Philosophy", in Freccero, 1965
—. "Dante's Idea of Love", in Bergin, 1967
—. *The Two Dantes*, London, 1977
W. Franke. *Dante's Interpretive Journey*, Chicago University Press, 1996
John Freccero. *Dante: The Poetics of Conversion,* ed. Rachel Jacoff, Harvard University Press, Cambridge, Mass., 1986
—. "Dante's Medusa: Allegory and Autobiography", in Jeffrey, 1979
—. ed. *Dante: A Collection of Critical Essays,* Prentice-Hall, Englewood Cliffs, 1965
Edmund Gardner. *Dante's Ten Heavens*, New York, 1970
John Guzzardo. "Number Symbolism in the *Vita Nuova*" , *Canadian Journal of Italian Studies*, 8, 30, 1985
Peter Hainsworth. "Cavalcanti in the *Vita Nuova*", *Modern Language Review,* 83, 1988
Robert P. Harrison. *The Body of Beatrice*, John Hopkins University Press, Baltimore, 1988
—. *Forests: The Shadow of Civilization*, University Press, 1992
Robert Hollander. "*Vita Nuova*: Dante's Perceptions of Beatrice", *Dante Studies*, 92, 1974
Julia B. Holloway. "The *Vita Nuova*: Paradigms of Pilgrimage", *Studies,* 103, 1985
George Holmes. *Dante*, Oxford University Press, 1980
Kay Howe. "Dante's Beatrice: The Nine and the Ten", *Italica*, 52, 1975
Amilcare A. Ianucci, ed. *Dante Today, Quaderni d'Italianistica*, 10, nos. 1-2, 1989
—. ed. *Dante: Contemporary Perspectives*, Toronto, 1995
Rachel Jacoff, ed. *The Cambridge Companion to Dante*, Cambridge University Press, 1993
—. ed. *Dante: The Poetics of Conversion*, Harvard University Press, Cambridge, Mass., 1986
—. "Transgression and Transcendence: Figures of Female Desire in Dante's *Commedia*", in Brownlee, 1991
—. "The Tears of Beatrice", *Dante Studies*, C, 1982
D.L. Jeffrey, ed. *By Things Seen: Reference and Recognition in Medieval Thought*, Ottawa, 1979
George Kay, ed. *The Penguin Book of Italian Verse*, Penguin, 1965
Sarah Kay & Miri Rubin, eds. *Framing Medieval Bodies*, Manchester University Press, 1996
Robin Kirkpatrick. *Dante's Inferno: Difficulty and Dead Poetry*, Cambridge University Press, 1987
—. "Dante and the Body", in Kay, 1996
J. Kleiner. "Finding the Center: Revelation and Reticence in the *Vita Nuova*", *Texas Studies in Literature and Language,* 32, 1, 1980
Christopher Kleinhenz. *The Early Italian Sonnet: The First Century (1220-1321),* Milella, Lecce, 1986
P.J. Klemp. "The Woman in the Middle: Layers of Love in Dante's *Vita Nuova*", *Italia*, 61, 3, 1984
Jerome Mazzaro. *The Figure of Dante: An Essay on the 'Vita Nuova',*

Princeton University Press, 1981

Joseph A. Mazzeo. *Medieval Cultural Tradition in Dante's 'Comedy'*, Cornell University Press, Ithaca, 1960

—. "Dante's Sun Symbolism", *Italica*, 33, Dec, 1956

Guiseppe Mazzotta. *Dante, Poet of the Desert: History and Allegory in 'The Divine Comedy'*, Princeton University Press, 1979

—. ed. *Critical Essays on Dante*, Hall, Boston, 1991

—. *Dante's Vision and the Circle of Knowledge,* Princeton University Press, 1992

—. "The Language of Poetry in the *Vita Nuova*", *Revisita di studi italini*, 1, 1983

Antonio C. Mastrobuono. *Dante's Journey of Sanctification,* Regnery Gateway, Washington DC, 1990

K. McKenzie. "The Symbolic Structure of Dante's *Vita Nuova*", *PMLA,* 18, 1903

Vincent Moleta. "The *Vita Nuova* as a Lyric Narrative", *Forum Italicum*, 12, 1978

Edward Moore. *Studies in Dante*, ed. Colin Hardie, 4 vols, Oxford University Press, 1968

Alison Morgan. *Dante and the Medieval Other World,* Cambridge University Press, 1990

Mark Musa. *Advent at the Gates: Dante's Comedy*, Indiana University Press, Bloomington, 1974

—. *Dante's* Vita Nuova: *A Translation and an Essay,* Indiana University Press, Bloomington, 1973

—. *Essays on Dante,* Indiana University Press, Bloomington, 1964

F.X. Newman, ed. *The Meaning of Courtly Love*, State University of New York Press, Albany, New York, 1968

Barbara Nolan. "The *Vita Nuova*: Dante's Book of Revelation", *Dante Studies*, 88, 1970

David Nolan, ed. *Dante Commentaries*, New Jersey, 1977

Charles Eliot Norton. *The New Life of Dante Alighieri*, Houghton-Mifflin, Boston 1895

Bernard O'Donoghue, ed. *The Courtly Love Tradition*, Manchester University Press, 1982

Francesco Petrarch. *Petrarch's Lyric Poems: the Rime Sparse and other Lyrics*, tr. Robert M. Durling, Harvard University Press, Cambridge, Mass., 1978

Michelanglo Picone. "Strutture poetiche e strutture prosastiche nella *Vita Nuova*", *Modern Language Notes*, 92, 1977

—. "La *Vita Nuova* e la tradizone poetica", *Dante Studies*, 95, 1977

—. "*Vita Nuova*" *e tradizione romanza*, Liviana Editrice, Padua, 1979

Arshi Pipa. "Personaggi della *Vita Nuova*: Dante, Cavalcanti e la famiglia Portinari", *Italica*, 62, 2, 1985

J.H. Potter. "Beatrice Dead or Alive: Love in the *Vita Nuova*", *Texas Studies in Literature and Language*, 32, 1990

Ricardo Quinones. *Dante Alighieri*, Twayne, Boston, 1979

J.A. Scott. "Dante's 'Sweet New Style' and the *Vita Nuova*", *Italica*, 42, 1965

93

—. *Woman Earthly and Divine in the Comedy of Dante*, Lexington, 1975

Charles Singleton. *An Essay on the Vita Nuova*, Harvard University Press, Cambridge, Mass., 1949

—. *Dante's 'Commedia': Elements of Structure, Dante Studies 1*, Harvard University Press, Cambridge, Mass., 1954

—. *Journey to Beatrice, Dante Studies 2*, Harvard University Press, Cambridge, Mass., 1958

Janet L. Smarr. "Celestial Patterns and Symmetries in the *Vita Nuova*", *Dante Studies*, 98, 1980

Michael R.G. Spiller. *The Development of the Sonnet: An Introduction*, Routledge, 1992

B. Stambler. *Dante's Other World*, New York University Press, 1957

Sara Sturm-Maddox. "The Pattern of Witness: Narrative Design in the *Vita Nuova*", *Forum Italicum*, 12, 1978

—. "Transformations of Courtly Poetry: *Vita Nuova* and *Canzoniere*", in Smith, 1980

David Thompson. *Dante's Epic Journeys*, John Hopkins University Press, Baltimore, 1974

J.F. Took. *Dante, Lyric Poet and Philosopher: An Introduction to the Minor Works*, Oxford University Press, 1990

Maurice Valency. *In Praise of Love: An Introduction to the Love-Poetry of the Renaissance*, Macmillan, New York, 1961

Nancy J. Vickers. "Diana described: scattered woman and scattered rhymes", *Critical Enquiry*, 8, 1981

Michel J. Viegnes. "Space and Love in the *Vita Nuova*", *Lectura Dantis*, 4, 1989

E.R. Vincent. "The Crisis in the *Vita Nuova*", *Century Essays on Dante by Members of the Oxford Dante Society*, Clarendon Press, 1965

David Wallace, ed. *Texas Studies in Literature and Language*, Spring, 1990

Life, Life
Selected Poems

Arseny Tarkovsky

translated and edited by Virginia Rounding

Arseny Tarkovsky is the neglected Russian poet, father of the acclaimed film director
Andrei Tarkovsky. This new book gathers together many of Tarkovsky's most lyrical
and heartfelt poems, in Rounding's clear, new translations. Many of Tarkovsky's poems
appeared in his son's films, such as *Mirror, Stalker, Nostalghia and The Sacrifice*.
There is an introduction by Rounding, and a bibliography of both Arseny and
Andrei Tarkovsky.

Bibliography and notes 124pp 3rd ed   ISBN 9781861712660 Hbk   ISBN 9781861711144

In the Dim Void

Samuel Beckett's Late Trilogy:
Company, Ill Seen, Ill Said and *Worstward Ho*

by Gregory Johns

This book discusses the luminous beauty and dense, rigorous poetry of Samuel Beckett's late works, *Company, Ill Seen, Ill Said* and *Worstward Ho*. Gregory Johns looks back over Beckett's long writing career, charting the development from the *Molloy-Malone Dies-Unnamable* trilogy through the 'fizzles' of the 1960s to the elegiac lyricism of the *Company* series. Johns compares the trilogy with late plays such as *Ghosts, Footfalls* and *Rockaby*.

Bibliography, notes. Illustrated. 120pp
ISBN 9781861712974 Pbk and ISBN 9781861712608 Hbk
9781861713407 E-book

Beauties, Beasts, and Enchantment

CLASSIC FRENCH FAIRY TALES

Translated and with an Introduction
by Jack Zipes

A collection of 36 classic French fairy tales translated by renowned writer Jack Zipes.
Cinderella, Beauty and the Beast, Sleeping Beauty and *Little Red Riding Hood* are among the
classic fairy tales in this amazing book.
Includes illustrations from fairy tale collections.
Jack Zipes has written and published widely on fairy tales.

'Terrific... a succulent array of 17th and 18th century 'salon' fairy tales'
- The New York Times Book Review

'These tales are adventurous, thrilling in a way fairy tales are meant to be... The translation
from the French is modern, happily free of archaic and hyperbolic language... a fine and
sophisticated collection' *- New York Tribune*

'Enjoyable to read... a unique collection of French regional folklore' *- Library Journal*

'Charming stories accompanied by attractive pen-and-ink drawings' *- Chattanooga Times*

Introduction and illustrations   612pp.   ISBN 9781861712510 Pbk   ISBN 9781861713193 Hbk

andy goldsworthy
touching nature

WILLIAM MALPAS

Contemporary British sculptor Andy Goldsworthy makes land and
environmental art, a sensitive, intuitive response to nature, light, time,
growth, change, the seasons and the earth. Goldsworthy's sculpture is
becoming ever more popular, appearing in TV documentaries, public works,
and Holocaust memorials. Goldsworthy has exhibited around the world, and
has become one of the foremost contemporary sculptors in Great Britain.

The book has been updated and revised for this new edition.

ISBN 9781861714122 Pbk   ISBN 9781861714138 Hbk
Fully illustrated   www.crmoon.com

CRESCENT MOON PUBLISHING

web: www.crmoon.com e-mail: cresmopub@yahoo.co.uk

ARTS, PAINTING, SCULPTURE

The Art of Andy Goldsworthy
Andy Goldsworthy: Touching Nature
Andy Goldsworthy in Close-Up
Andy Goldsworthy: Pocket Guide
Andy Goldsworthy In America
Land Art: A Complete Guide
The Art of Richard Long
Richard Long: Pocket Guide
Land Art In the UK
Land Art in Close-Up
Land Art In the U.S.A.
Land Art: Pocket Guide
Installation Art in Close-Up
Minimal Art and Artists In the 1960s and After
Colourfield Painting
Land Art DVD, TV documentary
Andy Goldsworthy DVD, TV documentary
The Erotic Object: Sexuality in Sculpture From Prehistory to the Present Day
Sex in Art: Pornography and Pleasure in Painting and Sculpture
Postwar Art
Sacred Gardens: The Garden in Myth, Religion and Art
Glorification: Religious Abstraction in Renaissance and 20th Century Art
Early Netherlandish Painting
Leonardo da Vinci
Piero della Francesca
Giovanni Bellini
Fra Angelico: Art and Religion in the Renaissance
Mark Rothko: The Art of Transcendence
Frank Stella: American Abstract Artist
Jasper Johns
Brice Marden
Alison Wilding: The Embrace of Sculpture
Vincent van Gogh: Visionary Landscapes
Eric Gill: Nuptials of God
Constantin Brancusi: Sculpting the Essence of Things
Max Beckmann
Caravaggio
Gustave Moreau
Egon Schiele: Sex and Death In Purple Stockings
Delizioso Fotografico Fervore: Works In Process 1
Sacro Cuore: Works In Process 2
The Light Eternal: J.M.W. Turner
The Madonna Glorified: Karen Arthurs

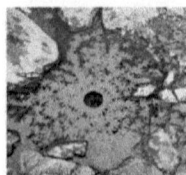

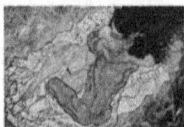

LITERATURE

J.R.R. Tolkien: The Books, The Films, The Whole Cultural Phenomenon
J.R.R. Tolkien: Pocket Guide
Tolkien's Heroic Quest
The *Earthsea* Books of Ursula Le Guin
Beauties, Beasts and Enchantment: Classic French Fairy Tales
German Popular Stories by the Brothers Grimm
Philip Pullman and *His Dark Materials*
Sexing Hardy: Thomas Hardy and Feminism
Thomas Hardy's *Tess of the d'Urbervilles*
Thomas Hardy's *Jude the Obscure*
Thomas Hardy: The Tragic Novels
Love and Tragedy: Thomas Hardy
The Poetry of Landscape in Hardy
Wessex Revisited: Thomas Hardy and John Cowper Powys
Wolfgang Iser: Essays and Interviews
Petrarch, Dante and the Troubadours
Maurice Sendak and the Art of Children's Book Illustration
Andrea Dworkin
Cixous, Irigaray, Kristeva: The *Jouissance* of French Feminism
Julia Kristeva: Art, Love, Melancholy, Philosophy, Semiotics and Psychoanalysis
Hélène Cixous I Love You: The *Jouissance* of Writing
Luce Irigaray: Lips, Kissing, and the Politics of Sexual Difference
Peter Redgrove: Here Comes the Flood
Peter Redgrove: Sex-Magic-Poetry-Cornwall
Lawrence Durrell: Between Love and Death, East and West
Love, Culture & Poetry: Lawrence Durrell
Cavafy: Anatomy of a Soul
German Romantic Poetry: Goethe, Novalis, Heine, Hölderlin
Feminism and Shakespeare
Shakespeare: Love, Poetry & Magic
The Passion of D.H. Lawrence
D.H. Lawrence: Symbolic Landscapes
D.H. Lawrence: Infinite Sensual Violence
Rimbaud: Arthur Rimbaud and the Magic of Poetry
The Ecstasies of John Cowper Powys
Sensualism and Mythology: The Wessex Novels of John Cowper Powys
Amorous Life: John Cowper Powys and the Manifestation of Affectivity (H.W. Fawkner)
Postmodern Powys: New Essays on John Cowper Powys (Joe Boulter)
Rethinking Powys: Critical Essays on John Cowper Powys
Paul Bowles & Bernardo Bertolucci
Rainer Maria Rilke
Joseph Conrad: *Heart of Darkness*
In the Dim Void: Samuel Beckett
Samuel Beckett Goes into the Silence
André Gide: Fiction and Fervour
Jackie Collins and the Blockbuster Novel
Blinded By Her Light: The Love-Poetry of Robert Graves
The Passion of Colours: Travels In Mediterranean Lands
Poetic Forms

POETRY

Ursula Le Guin: Walking In Cornwall
Peter Redgrove: Here Comes The Flood
Peter Redgrove: Sex-Magic-Poetry-Cornwall
Dante: Selections From the Vita Nuova
Petrarch, Dante and the Troubadours
William Shakespeare: Sonnets
William Shakespeare: Complete Poems
Blinded By Her Light: The Love-Poetry of Robert Graves
Emily Dickinson: Selected Poems
Emily Brontë: Poems
Thomas Hardy: Selected Poems
Percy Bysshe Shelley: Poems
John Keats: Selected Poems
Joh n Keats: Poems of 1820
D.H. Lawrence: Selected Poems
Edmund Spenser: Poems
Edmund Spenser: Amoretti
John Donne: Poems
Henry Vaughan: Poems
Sir Thomas Wyatt: Poems
Robert Herrick: Selected Poems
Rilke: Space, Essence and Angels in the Poetry of Rainer Maria Rilke
Rainer Maria Rilke: Selected Poems
Friedrich Hölderlin: Selected Poems
Arseny Tarkovsky: Selected Poems
Arthur Rimbaud: Selected Poems
Arthur Rimbaud: A Season in Hell
Arthur Rimbaud and the Magic of Poetry
Novalis: Hymns To the Night
German Romantic Poetry
Paul Verlaine: Selected Poems
Elizaethan Sonnet Cycles
D.J. Enright: By-Blows
Jeremy Reed: Brigitte's Blue Heart
Jeremy Reed: Claudia Schiffer's Red Shoes
Gorgeous Little Orpheus
Radiance: New Poems
Crescent Moon Book of Nature Poetry
Crescent Moon Book of Love Poetry
Crescent Moon Book of Mystical Poetry
Crescent Moon Book of Elizabethan Love Poetry
Crescent Moon Book of Metaphysical Poetry
Crescent Moon Book of Romantic Poetry
Pagan America: New American Poetry

MEDIA, CINEMA, FEMINISM and CULTURAL STUDIES

J.R.R. Tolkien: The Books, The Films, The Whole Cultural Phenomenon
J.R.R. Tolkien: Pocket Guide
The *Lord of the Rings* Movies: Pocket Guide
The Cinema of Hayao Miyazaki
Hayao Miyazaki: *Princess Mononoke*: Pocket Movie Guide
Hayao Miyazaki: *Spirited Away*: Pocket Movie Guide
Tim Burton : Hallowe'en For Hollywood
Ken Russell
Ken Russell: *Tommy*: Pocket Movie Guide
The Ghost Dance: The Origins of Religion
The Peyote Cult
Cixous, Irigaray, Kristeva: The *Jouissance* of French Feminism
Julia Kristeva: Art, Love, Melancholy, Philosophy, Semiotics and Psychoanalysis
Luce Irigaray: Lips, Kissing, and the Politics of Sexual Difference
Hélene Cixous I Love You: The *Jouissance* of Writing
Andrea Dworkin
'Cosmo Woman': The World of Women's Magazines
Women in Pop Music
HomeGround: The Kate Bush Anthology
Discovering the Goddess (Geoffrey Ashe)
The Poetry of Cinema
The Sacred Cinema of Andrei Tarkovsky
Andrei Tarkovsky: Pocket Guide
Andrei Tarkovsky: *Mirror*: Pocket Movie Guide
Andrei Tarkovsky: *The Sacrifice*: Pocket Movie Guide
Walerian Borowczyk: Cinema of Erotic Dreams
Jean-Luc Godard: The Passion of Cinema
Jean-Luc Godard: *Hail Mary*: Pocket Movie Guide
Jean-Luc Godard: *Contempt*: Pocket Movie Guide
Jean-Luc Godard: *Pierrot le Fou*: Pocket Movie Guide
John Hughes and Eighties Cinema
Ferris Bueller's Day Off: Pocket Movie Guide
Jean-Luc Godard: Pocket Guide
The Cinema of Richard Linklater
Liv Tyler: Star In Ascendance
Blade Runner and the Films of Philip K. Dick
Paul Bowles and Bernardo Bertolucci
Media Hell: Radio, TV and the Press
An Open Letter to the BBC
Detonation Britain: Nuclear War in the UK
Feminism and Shakespeare
Wild Zones: Pornography, Art and Feminism
Sex in Art: Pornography and Pleasure in Painting and Sculpture
Sexing Hardy: Thomas Hardy and Feminism

The Light Eternal is a model monograph, an exemplary job. The subject matter of the book is beautifully
organised and dead on beam. (Lawrence Durrell)
It is amazing for me to see my work treated with such passion and respect. (Andrea Dworkin)

CRESCENT MOON PUBLISHING
P.O. Box 1312, Maidstone, Kent, ME14 5XU, Great Britain. www.crmoon.com

cresmopub@yahoo.co.uk   www.crescentmoon.org.uk

www.ingramcontent.com/pod-product-compliance
Lightning Source LLC
Chambersburg PA
CBHW061835040426
42447CB00012B/2983